KID'S TRAVEL GUIDE TO
NEW YORK CITY

A MUST HAVE TRAVEL BOOK FOR KIDS WITH BEST PLACES TO VISIT, FUN FACTS, ACTIVITIES, GAMES, AND MORE!

Dylanna Travel Press

Published by Dylanna Travel Guides an imprint of Dylanna Publishing, Inc.

Copyright © 2019 by Dylanna Travel Guides

Editor: Julie Grady

All rights reserved. No part of this publication may be reproduced, stored in a retrieval system, or transmitted by any means, including electronic, mechanical, photocopying, or otherwise, without prior written permission of the publisher.

Although the publisher has taken all reasonable care in the preparation of this book, we make no warranty about the accuracy or completeness of its content and, to the maximum extent permitted, disclaim all liability arising from its use.

Printed in the U.S.A.

TABLE OF CONTENTS

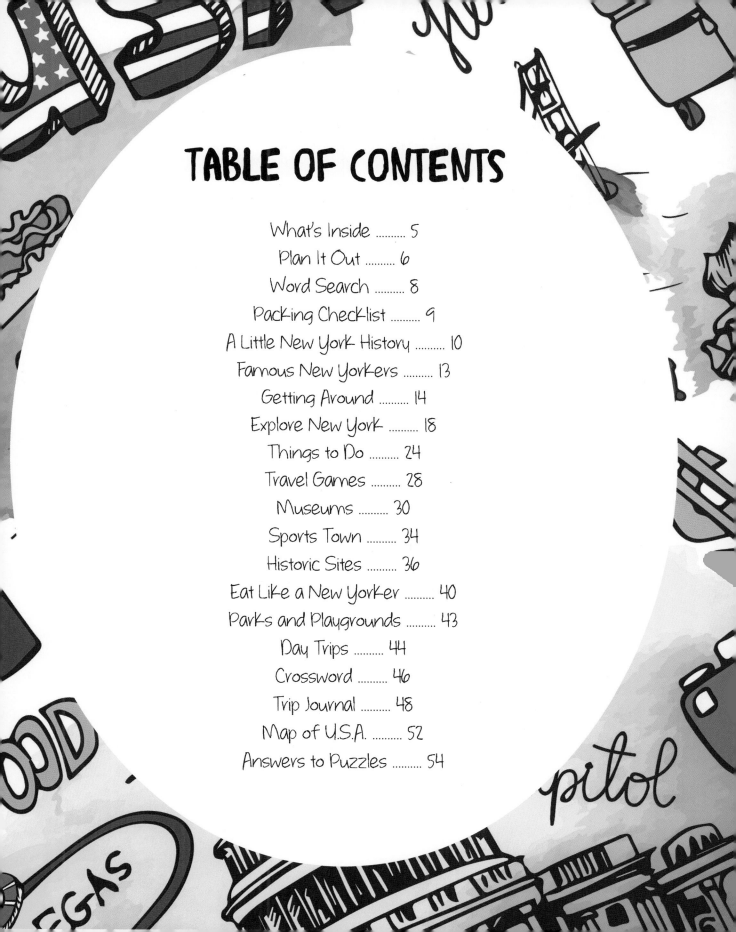

Congratulations, You've Going on a Trip to New York City!

Planning and going on a trip is an exciting adventure. This **Kid's Guide and Activity Book** is going to help you get ready for, and have loads of fun on, your journey.

What's Inside

Packed inside this book is lots of information about places to see and things to do while you're in New York City, as well as entertaining games and activities to get you excited about your trip. Along with fun facts and puzzles there's also plenty of room to record your own memories.

=> Getting Ready for Your Trip
=> Interesting Historical Facts and Sites
=> Top Places to Visit and Things to Do
=> Cool Museums
=> Neighborhoods to Explore
=> Best Ways to Get Around
=> Signature Foods to Try
=> Day Trips
=> Games and Activities

Ready? Let's Go!

PLAN IT OUT

When are we leaving? _____
_____
_____
_____
_____
_____

Who's going? _____
_____
_____
_____

How are we getting there? _____
_____
_____
_____

What I'm most looking forward to: _____
_____
_____
_____
_____

AIRPORT

Word Search

```
S H I R T H S S N E A K E R S
F B Y Q O O R U G H S Z A S F
C H A R G E R U N T Q L U N I
A W P R T C G G R S L H U A B
A L A R O V A O J E C S N C Y
Z B C Q O M H M R O E R H K Q
Z P K G T S W B E H U E E S B
B A I S H T M S T R S R T E J
L N N H B U R O A A A E N Q N
X T G A R D L A C N K B I A T
M S S M U C Z T V C D G V D L
G S V P S F I T A E D A G V U
U Y W O H U V J O Z L Z L X D
B I D O S P A J A M A S Z S E
S U N G L A S S E S Y L U O I
```

CAMERA	PANTS	SUITCASE
CHARGER	SANDALS	SUNGLASSES
CLOTHES	SHAMPOO	SUNSCREEN
JACKET	SHIRT	TOOTHBRUSH
JOURNAL	SHORTS	TRAVEL
PACKING	SNACKS	UMBRELLA
PAJAMAS	SNEAKERS	

PACKING CHECKLIST

CLOTHES

- [ ] T-Shirts
- [ ] Long-sleeved Shirts
- [ ] Sweatshirts and Sweaters
- [ ] Pants
- [ ] Shorts
- [ ] Jacket/Raincoat
- [ ] Underwear
- [ ] Pajamas
- [ ] Socks
- [ ] Bathing Suit/ Cover-Up
- [ ] Sneakers
- [ ] Shoes/Sandals
- [ ] Dressy Outfit
- [ ]

PERSONAL ITEMS

- [ ] Soap
- [ ] Toothbrush/Toothpaste/Floss
- [ ] Shampoo/Conditioner
- [ ] Brush/Comb
- [ ] Glasses/Contacts
- [ ]

TRAVEL ITEMS

- [ ] Book/Audio Book
- [ ] Drinks/Snacks
- [ ] Charger
- [ ] Phone/Tablet/Camera
- [ ] Headphones
- [ ] Notepad/Journal
- [ ] Pen/Pencil
- [ ] This Guide Book
- [ ]

MISCELLANEOUS

- [ ] Sunscreen
- [ ] Umbrella
- [ ] Batteries
- [ ] Hand wipes
- [ ]
- [ ]
- [ ]

9

A Little New York History

New York City, also known as the Big Apple, is the largest city in the United states with a population of 8 million people.

Originally called New Amsterdam, it was first discovered by Europeans in the 1500s and was settled by the Dutch in 1609. Dutch settlers bought the land from Native Americans.

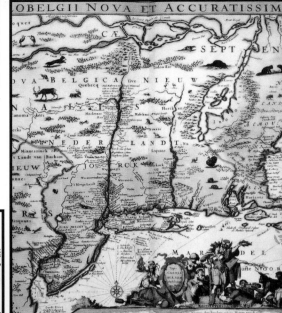

The English took over governance in 1664, after the Anglo-Dutch War, and changed the name to New York after the Duke of York (later King James II of England).

The city's prime location made it a target for the British during the Revolutionary War and many battles were fought here including the Battle of Harlem Heights. It was controlled by the British until 1783 and was a haven for Loyalists (those loyal to the British during the American Revolution).

Sergev Gorvachev / Shutterstock.com

After the Revolutionary War, under the Articles of Confederation, New York was the first capital of the United States from 1785 to 1790.

Due to its central location, with rail, steamboat, and coastal connections, the city became the foremost port on the Atlantic coast during the nineteenth century.

Millions of immigrants arrived in the 1800s and early 1900s, changing the ethnic composition of the city and leading to even greater industrial expansion. Many immigrants arrived through Ellis Island.

In 1898, the five boroughs joined to form New York City, giving the city the modern composition we know today. New York continued to grow following the Great Depression and World War II.

Today, New York City is one of the most influential cities, both culturally and economically, in the world.

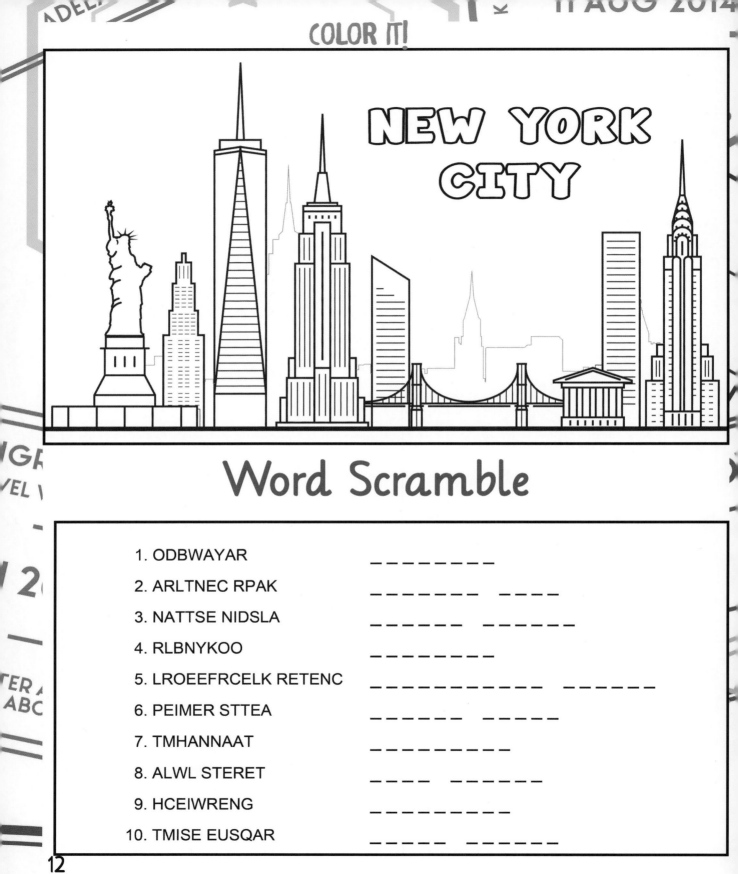

COLOR IT!

NEW YORK CITY

Word Scramble

1. ODBWAYAR   _ _ _ _ _ _ _ _
2. ARLTNEC RPAK   _ _ _ _ _ _   _ _ _ _
3. NATTSE NIDSLA   _ _ _ _ _ _   _ _ _ _ _ _
4. RLBNYKOO   _ _ _ _ _ _ _ _
5. LROEEFRCELK RETENC _ _ _ _ _ _ _ _ _ _   _ _ _ _ _ _
6. PEIMER STTEA   _ _ _ _ _ _   _ _ _ _ _
7. TMHANNAAT   _ _ _ _ _ _ _ _ _
8. ALWL STERET   _ _ _ _   _ _ _ _ _ _
9. HCEIWRENG   _ _ _ _ _ _ _ _ _
10. TMISE EUSQAR   _ _ _ _ _   _ _ _ _ _ _

12

Famous New Yorkers

Many famous people have called New York home.

Walt Whitman (1810-1892) – Poet, essayist, and journalist. His most famous work is Leaves of Grass.

Frederick Douglass (1818-1895) – Former slave who became a leader of abolitionist movement, author, and editor the newspaper The North Star.

Susan B. Anthony (1820-1906) – Social reformer, abolitionist, and women's rights activist. One of the leaders of the women's suffrage movement.

Theodore Roosevelt (1858-1919) – After the assassination of President McKinley, Roosevelt became the 26th President of the United States. A leader of the Progressive Era..

catwalker / Shutterstock.com

Franklin D. Roosevelt (1882-1945) – FDR was the 32nd President of the United States. President during the Great Depression, he established the New Deal.

catwalker / Shutterstock.com

Ogden Nash (1902-1971) – Well-known poet who wrote over 500 poems including many humorous and light-hearted poems.

catwalker / Shutterstock.com

Lou Gehrig (1903-1941) – Baseball player for the New York Yankees. Nicknamed the "Iron Horse." Played on six World Series champion teams and is in the Baseball Hall of Fame.

DFree / Shutterstock.com

Spike Lee (1957-) – Film director, producer, and actor. Has made over 35 films including BlacKkKlansman, Malcolm X, and Do the Right Thing.

Featureflash Photo Agency / Shutterstock.com

Christina Aguilera (1980-) – Singer and songwriter. Time magazine named her one of their 100 most influential people in the world.

Anne Hathaway (1982-) – Actress and singer. Won an Academy Award for her role in Les Miserables. One of highest-paid actors in the world. **13**

IStone / Shutterstock.com

Getting Around

Walk It!

New York has been rated the most walkable city in the United States and walking is a great way to get around and explore. Plus this is an excellent way to get some exercise and discover those hidden gems.

With so many neighborhoods and parks to explore, you will never get tired of wandering around this fabulous city. Need a break? Relax in the shade on a bench in Central Park or stop at one of the many sidewalk cafes for a refreshing drink and a bite to eat.

Hail a Cab!

Don't feel like walking? Taxis are one of the most convenient ways of getting around the city. To hail a cab look for one with its light on, raise your hand, and yell "taxi"!

Luciano Mortula - LGM / Shutterstock.com

Take the Subway

The New York Metropolitan Tranportation Authority (MTA) operates the subway and buslines. The subway is an inexpensive and fast way of getting around quickly. It provides access to all of the five boroughs and operates 24 hours a day, seven days a week. The fare is $2.75 or you can buy a multi-use MetroCard.

Metropolitan Transportation Authority of the State of New York [CC BY 2.0 (https://creativecommons.org/licenses/by/2.0)]

Map of New York

Explore New York
Geography and Neighborhoods

New York City, aka the Big Apple, is divided into different boroughs and neighborhoods, each with a distinctive personality.

Upper East Side – Home to many of the cities ultra-wealthy, the Upper East Side is where you will find "Museum Mile" including the Metropolitan Museum of Art and the Guggenheim Museum. There are many restaurants here, from fine dining to casual diners, or do some shopping along ritzy Madison Avenue.

Upper West Side – Bordering Central Park and with brownstone-lined streets, this neighborhood is home to several popular museums including the American Museum of Natural History and the Children's Museum of Manhattan, as well as Lincoln Center.

Tinnaporn Sathapornnanont / Shutterstock.com

Flatiron District/Union Square – The landmark Flatiron Building gives this neighborhood its name. Union Square is a popular spot for street performers and skateboarders, as well as being home to the well-known Union Square Greenmarket.

Midtown – This is one of the busiest areas of New York. Many tourist attractions are located here including Times Square, Rockefeller Center, St. Patrick's Cathedral, and the Empire State Building. Come here to see the sights, lights, and crowds of New York.

Luciano Mortula - LGM / Shutterstock.com

Chelsea – This artists' district has over 300 art galleries. It is also full of great restaurants, shops, and cultural activities. Chelsea is where you will find High Line Park, a bit of greenery in the city built on an abandoned railroad track.

Nicole Kwiatkowski / Shutterstock.com

Everett Collection / Shutterstock.com

Harlem – Historically the center of African American culture, this neighborhood is home to the famous Apollo Theater. This multicultural neighborhood is currently undergoing a revitalization.

Wall Street/Financial District – The oldest part of Manhattan, the Financial District has many historic sites and museums, including 1 World Trade Center and the 9/11 Memorial and Museum. This is also the neighborhood for access to the Statue of Liberty, Ellis Island, and the Brooklyn Bridge.

photo.ua / Shutterstock.com

travelview / Shutterstock.com

Chinatown – For a taste of China in New York, head to Chinatown. Here you can expect crowded sidewalks, lots of stores, and authentic Asian restaurants. Chinatown continues to expand and has taken over much of Little Italy and the Lower East Side.

DW labs Incorporated / Shutterstock.com

SoHo and Tribeca – These are two of the trendiest neighborhoods in New York, famous for high-end shopping (check out Broadway), and fancy restaurants. Many of the best hotels can be found in this area.

Greenwich Village – Also known as "The Village," this is one of the more desirable neighborhoods to live in. Check out the yummy bakeries located here and maybe spot a few celebrities.

JJFarq / Shutterstock.com

rblfmr / Shutterstock.com

East Village – A colorful neighborhood located east of the Bowery and Third Avenue, with Houston Street in the south and 14th Street in the north, this eclectic neighborhood is full of cafes, shops, and ethnic restaurants.

Hell's Kitchen – Also called Clinton, this neighborhood is on the West Side of Midtown with 59th Street to the north and 34th Street to the south. This diverse neighborhood is bustling with energy and character. Head there to check out the Flea Market filled with eclectic wares, it is a bargain shoppers delight.

Sean Pavone / Shutterstock.com

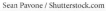

JJFarq / Shutterstock.com

Little Italy – For authentic Italian cuisine there's no better place in the city than Little Italy, the former haven for Italian immigrants in New York. The narrow streets and vintage Italian storefronts still retain their old-world charm.

Connect the Dots and Color!

23

Top Places to See and Things to Do

Statue of Liberty – An iconic must see when visiting New York City. A great way to get a good view is to take a ride on the Staten Island Ferry. This free ferry takes you on a 25-minute one-way ride and provides views of New York Harbor and the Statue of Liberty. If you want to spend more time, take a tour that includes a visit to Ellis Island.

Central Park – A green oasis in the heart of Manhattan, this 843 acre park is perfect for families. Central Park is full of things that kids love including the Central Park Carousel, the Central Park Zoo, Tisch Children's Zoo, gondola rides, model boat sailing, twenty-one playgrounds, and, if you're visiting in winter, ice skating. Visit the official Central Park website to find out what is happening in the park during your visit.

stockelements / Shutterstock.com

Rockefeller Center – Historic landmark in the heart of Midtown Manhattan. Take the elevator to the Top of the Rock Observation Deck for spectacular views of the city. Other attractions here include ice skating rink, Radio City Stage Door tour, NBC Studios tour, and the iconic Christmas Tree.

Luciano Mortula - LGM / Shutterstock.com

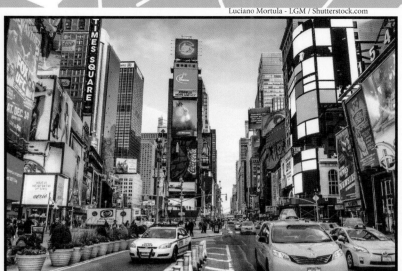

Times Square – A major tourist destination right in the heart of Midtown. It's crowded, noisy, bright, and unforgettable. Located at the intersection of 7th Avenue and Broadway, many popular attractions are located in and around this area including Madame Tussauds, Ripley's Believe It or Not, M&M World, LEGO Store, Dylan's Candy, Top of the Rock, Gulliver's Gate, and more!

Empire State Building – Completed in 1931, this Art Deco-style skyscraper is 102 stories tall and is the fifth-tallest skyscraper in the country. Located in Midtown Manhattan, this symbol of New York is a National Historic Landmark and has been featured in countless films and television shows. Visitors can visit the Observation Deck located on the 102nd floor which provides 360-degree views of New York City.

Cedric Weber / Shutterstock.com

anderm / Shutterstock.com

9/11 Memorial and Museum – Remember and honor the 2,983 people who lost their lives in the terrorist acts of September 11, 2001. Exhibitions and educational programs.

25

One World Observatory – Experience the thrill of riding one of the fastest elevators in the world to the top of the tallest building in the USA. The views from the top are amazing and there are videos and interactive displays that provide a panoramic view of the city.

Leonard Zhukovsky / Shutterstock.com

Bronx Zoo – The largest urban zoo in the country, the Bronx Zoo spreads out over 265 acres and is home to more than 600 different species. Open year round.

New York Botanical Garden – Enjoy this oasis in the city any time of the year. Located in the Bronx, this 240-acre botanical garden features more than a million plants. Be sure to check out the Everett Children's Adventure Garden where you can climb the boulders, check out the lily pads, or explore your way through a maze. Open year round.

Leonard Zhukovsky / Shutterstock.com

Sightseeing Tours – A great way to explore New York City, as well as learn some interesting facts, it to take a sightseeing tour. One of the more popular tours are the hop-on, hop-off bus tours run by several different companies. These tours stop at most of the popular locations throughout the city and allow you to jump off and explore wherever you wish.

Broadway – If you can, take in a Broadway show while visiting NYC, the most famous theater district in the world. Cheap, last-minute tickets can often be found on the day of the show. Popular shows for families include the Lion King, Wicked, Frozen, and Aladdin.

Sociopath987 / Shutterstock.com

dmitro2009 / Shutterstock.com

Central Park Zoo – Located inside Central Park, here you will find more than 130 different species from penguins to grizzly bears. Five acres designed to recreate a variety of habitats and environments.

27

Travel Crossword

Across

2. The place you go at the end of your trip.
5. Bring this type of book with you when you travel.
6. A green area in a city for people to enjoy.
8. The place you go to catch a plane.
9. The number of states in the United States.
10. A type of public transportation that is underground.
11. The thing you carry your belongings in when you travel.

Down

1. Say good _____ when you leave.
2. Another word for vacation.
3. Look at this when you are lost to figure out where to go.
4. When you travel by _____ you might run into traffic.
7. Mode of transportation to get from place to place fast.

Find the Travel Icons in the Picture

A Day at the Museum

Want to learn something and have fun doing it?
Check out these top museums in New York City.

Metropolitan Museum of Art – One of the world's largest and best art museums. Contains more than 2 million works of art in its collection. A great place to explore art and experience fun, interactive programs. Check out the Family Tours.

littlenySTOCK / Shutterstock.com

Luis War / Shutterstock.com

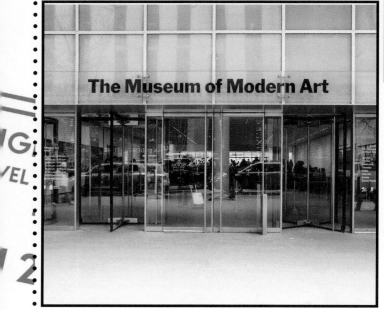

Museum of Modern Art – This art museum is located right in Midtown. It contains one of the finest collections of contemporary art from the eighteen century through today. Here you can see Van Gogh's Starry Night as well as Picasso's Les Demoiselles d'Avignon and Salvador Dali's The Persistence of Memory.

Manuel Ochoa / Shutterstock.com

Guggenheim Museum – Located on the Upper East Side, this museum houses a spectacular collection of modern art. In addition, the building itself is a work of art, designed by famed architect Frank Lloyd Wright. Take the elevator to the top of the museum and work your way down through the winding spiral.

Osugi / Shutterstock.com

Whitney Museum of American Art –

This museum is dedicated to showcasing the works of American artists. Famous artists shown here include Edward Hopper, Georgia O'Keefe, and Alexander Calder.

Clari Massimiliano / Shutterstock.com

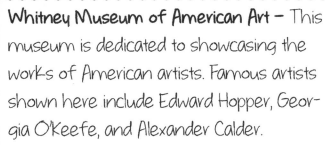

American Museum of Natural History –

This is the museum featured in the film Night at the Museum and is one of the world's best. The dinosaur collection, including the T-rex, is a must see, as well as exhibits focusing on biodiversity, ocean life, and the planetarium.

Pavel L Photo and Video / Shutterstock.com

South Street Seaport Museum

– Anyone interested in boats, shipping, and maritime history should head over to the South Street Seaport Museum. Here you can explore historic ships, use a letterpress, or take a sail around New York Harbor.

Trip to the Museum Word Search

```
E B G A H I S T O R Y V R S Z T I S I V
M S K Q R Z J W A T P J O D I R T C K F
E S O R Q C D Q X A G R L Q I B Y A B U
E O H Y V C H L W P U E E K T O E K A D
C Q J N T Y C I M K I X M S M A E Z S O
N T O O E S L I V Z D H U Y E S F U C V
E S A I D G P A Q E E I E J B R D Y Z G
I W R S G A T S C F S B S I E G V N Y W
C V T S F P W M O V S I U P G S C E W G
S V I I O G H T L D R T M L G Z E G N K
X D F M S M U I R A T E N A L P E I V E
Z P A D S B P N G M Q G I I D U T F D W
U O C A I D W T Y L N D D N E N M Y P E
S I T P L G D F I O L R L E I H K O A R
Y C S I S L M O Y C U D T A V S H C O Z
K O B A E H B P T A K V P Q D S T T L B
A R T I S T M C T J T E N U T M A O S T
C O L L E C T I O N Z I T F E R T F U D
N T T G W Q Z V K Q Y D I F U O W C I R
O O I G N I N R A E L G R C D M D D P U
```

ADMISSION	CURATOR	HISTORY	PRESERVE
ARCHIVES	EXHIBIT	LEARNING	SCIENCE
ARTIFACTS	FOSSILS	MUSEUM	TICKET
ARTIST	GIFT SHOP	PAINTING	TOUR
COLLECTION	GUIDE	PLANETARIUM	VISIT

Children's Museum of the Arts

– This kid-centered art museum features hands-on activities, art workshops, and more than 2,000 works of art, many created by kids.

Pit Stock / Shutterstock.com

New York City Fire Museum

– If you're a kid who likes firetrucks (and who isn't?) then check out this museum located in a historic firehouse. Learn about the history of firefighters, see vintage fire equipment, and get fire safety tips.

Ritu Manoj Jethani / Shutterstock.com

Children's Museum of Manhattan

– Hands-on learning dedicated to creating fun and interesting experiences for kids. Five floors of interactive, rotating exhibits. Located on the Upper West Side.

Intrepid Sea, Air & Space Museum

– Explore the legendary aircraft carrier, Intrepid, the space shuttle Enterprise, a guided missile submarine, and the world's fastest jets. In Exploreum, you can climb in a real helicopter and even practice landing a space shuttle.

Tupungato / Shutterstock.com

Sports Town!

New York is a sports town and there's nothing New Yorkers love more than rooting for their favorite teams. If you can while you are visiting go to a game. Depending on the season, head over to Yankee Stadium in the Bronx, go to a Knicks' or Ranger' game at Madison Square Garden, or take a drive to MetLife Stadium to see the Giants or the Jets.

GagliardiPhotography / Shutterstock.com

littlenySTOCK / Shutterstock.com

Yankee Stadium has been the home of the New York Yankees since 1923 . You can take a behind-the-scenes tour of this famous ballpark and learn the history of the 27-time World Series winning champs.

Both the NY Knicks and the NY Rangers play at **Madison Square Garden.**

Christopher Penler / Shutterstock.com

Christopher Penler / Shutterstock.com

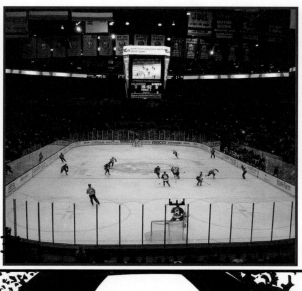

MetLife Stadium, located 11 miles from NYC in New Jersey, is where you can see the New York Giants and Jets play football.

Sports Trivia

1. Where is the basketball hall of fame located? _____

2. For what team did Babe Ruth play for? _____

3. In what sport is the Stanley Cup given out? _____

4. What year was baseball invented in? _____

5. Where is Fenway Park located? _____

6. What is the original home of the LA Dodgers? _____

7. Which sport does not use a ball? _____

8. What city hosted the 2002 Winter Olympics? _____

9. What three events are in a triathlon? _____

10. How long is a marathon? _____

11. Which sports play on a court? _____

12. In what sport do you need a caddy? _____

13. The Tour de France is what type of event?_____

14. What is another name for ping pong? _____

See Some Historic Sites

Kamira / Shutterstock.com

Brooklyn Bridge – One of the oldest suspension bridges in the United States (finished in 1883) and first steel-wire bridge in the world. Connects Brooklyn and Manhattan across the East River. It takes approximately 30 minutes to walk the 1.3 miles across the bridge.

pisaphotography / Shutterstock.com

St. Patrick's Cathedral – A neo-Gothic style church located in Midtown directly across from Rockefeller Center. Work began on the cathedral in 1858 and continued until 1906. It has a beautiful marble façade, stained glass windows, and magnificent art works.

Flatiron Building – Built in 1902, architect Daniel Burnham designed its distinctive triangular shape. Located at the intersection of Fifth Avenue and Broadway, it is an iconic New York City landmark.

V_E / Shutterstock.com

Grand Central Terminal – First built in 1871 by robber baron Cornelius Vanderbilt, Grand Central Station has been through many transformations. Today, in addition to being a busy commuter hub, it also hosts many special events as well as art and cultural exhibits.

Apollo Theater – Located in Harlem, this historic theater is most famously associated with African American performers and the Harlem Renaissance. Built in 1913, it showcased black entertainers throughout the twentieth century including Ella Fitzgerald and Billie Holiday.

Everett Collection / Shutterstock.com

Warren Eisenberg / Shutterstock.com

Joseph Sohm / Shutterstock.com

Theodore Roosevelt Birthplace National Historic Site – Childhood home of the twenty-sixth president of the United States. The current structure is a reconstruction of the original 1848 home that was demolished in 1916.

Felix Lipov / Shutterstock.com

Woolworth Building – Located at 233 Broadway, the Woolworth Building was once the tallest building in the world. Designed by architect Cass Gilbert, construction on the building was completed in 1913. Today the building is used as offices, residences, and commercial space.

Chrysler Building – This Art Deco style skyscraper is located at the corner of Lexington Avenue and 42nd Street. Completed in 1930, this 1,046-foot tall building was once the tallest building in the world until it was overtaken by the Empire State Building.

Federal Hall National Memorial – New York was the first capital of the United States and this is where the first Congress met and wrote the Bill of Rights. In addition, George Washington was inaugurated here as the first president of the United States. Currently the building is a museum and memorial to the early years of our country.

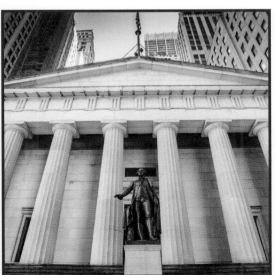

Ellis Island – More than 12 million immigrants entered the United States through Ellis Island between 1892 and 1954. Located in New York Harbor, this small island was the first federal immigration station.

New York City Word Search

```
Y R R E F Q E N J H W P K W L U T P R W
B Q S U C U L O Y J G M R C Y F A T S A
Z E W A Q S O T L W M E A O N Y X B C L
J J Q B U W E E U F S B P S Y T I D V L
O V B E C X K E L M S V L M G R S Z W S
L R A Q U Z N C J N A I A Q C E P R T T
B N W F T H P D O G E M R E A B Y P L R
E R A U Q S S E M I T Q T N N I T S A E
P Q B K K N K Z N O J J N B I L G E N E
X Y R H X Z A C Q A V P E H O W B A A T
F X O J Y N S F D X I F C I C N D P T K
A U O Y A N K E E S R X P D C K D O T X
W Z K V G U G G E N H E I M A V Z R A V
D U L P G A U W Y A W D A O R B C T H E
Y T Y L K A I Y T D H J C T Z E I T N W
L C N F R S Z Z G I K W I Z Z Y J T A Z
N Z Z C M N G R E E N W I C H R Q O M T
C H V Z C A P X X W A Y S S F D R Q J I
C K M E L R A H G R Z O O Q Y I B I D E
O G Z N Q P H E B A F O Y O J Y A J J J
```

BROADWAY	GUGGENHEIM	TAXIS
BROOKLYN	HARLEM	TIMES SQUARE
CENTRAL PARK	LIBERTY	WALL STREET
FERRY	MANHATTAN	YANKEES
GREENWICH	SEAPORT	ZOO

Eat Like a New Yorker

When in New York be sure to try some of the signature dishes that it is known for like New York-style pizza and spectacular desserts.

Manhattan Clam Chowder – Unlike its creamier cousin, New England Clam Chowder, Manhattan-style chowder is a tomato-based chowder filled with clams, pork, potatoes, and other vegetables.

Bagels – Authentic New York bagels are like no other. Thick and crusty on the outside and fluffy on the inside, you'll find them in many flavors including sesame seeds, poppy seeds, onion, raisin, or pumpernickel. Top with butter, cream cheese, smoked fish, or just eat them plain.

Pastrami on Rye – There's nothing more New York than pastrami on rye. Head over to the world-famous Jewish deli, Katz's Delicatessen, for this classic sandwich of pastrami and mustard on rye bread.

Leonard Zhukovsky / Shutterstock.com

Potato Knish – This Yiddish dumpling has a potato filling inside and a thick dough that is either baked or fried. Find them at diners, delis, and street vendors all over New York.

Pretzels – Street cart pretzels are available all over New York City and are a favorite food that can be eaten on the run. Warm, soft, salted, and deliciously baked – who can resist?

ChameleonsEye / Shutterstock.com

Pizza – New York-style pizza is world famous. If you can, visit Lombardi's the first pizzeria in the United States. Or, pick up a "dollar slice" at 2 Bros. Pizza.

Hot Dogs – Grab a delicious New York hot dog for a quick and easy lunch. Hot dogs should be crispy on the outside and juicy on the inside. Top with onions, relish, mustard, or whatever you fancy.

Gnocchi – New Yorkers love the type of pasta known as gnocchi, and it is served up at restaurants all across the city.

Black and White Cookies – Surprise, those famous black and whites are really not cookies at all! They are really little cakes that are then frosted with half vanilla and half chocolate frosting. Delicious!

New York-Style Cheesecake – Rich, creamy, and so delicious, there's nothing like a slice of New York cheesecake. Try it at Junior's, a New York institution, and top it with fresh fruit.

41

Parks and Playgrounds

When you need a little break, head over to one of New York's many parks and playgrounds (over 1,700!) to relax, run around, and let off some steam.

=> Central Park – There are many fun playgrounds to check out within Central Park including Ancient Playground – located near the Metropolitan Museum of Art, this playground contains pyramids, a sundial, and an obelisk inspired by Egyptian Art ; Billy Johnson Playground – with its 45-foot granite slide, lush plantings, and rustic structures; Heckscher Playground – the oldest and largest playground in Central Park, it's got plenty of ramps, slides, and tunnels to explore.

=>Imagination Playground – This interactive play space was designed to stimulate creative free play. There are sand and water features, as well as giant foam blocks and mats.

=> Chelsea Waterside Park – This recently renovated playground in Hudson River Park includes sprinklers, a giant 64-foot slide, and a large sandpit.

=> Children's Adventure Garden – Part of the New York Botanical Garden, this playspace offers boulders to climb, mazes to run through, and hands-on science activities.

=> The High Line – This elevated public park on the West Side was previously a freight rail line. One and a half miles long, the park meanders through several neighborhoods. Walk through gardens, check out the artwork, grab a bite from a food vendor, or play on Pershing Square Beams, a playground constructed from the original railroad framework.

Day Trips

If you have time while in the New York area, check out some of these amazing places that are only a short distance away.

Cape May, NJ – If you want to have some fun and sun, then head out to Cape May, located 2 1/2 hours from New York City. This quaint seaside town has beautiful beaches, whale watching, biking, swimming, and hiking.

Hamptons, NY – Ready for a day at the beach? A 2 1/2 hour drive from New York City, the Hamptons are packed with family friendly activities. After the beach, play some mini-golf, go to a local baseball game, or see a puppet show at the Goat on a Boat Puppet Theatre. Or rent bikes and just explore some trails.

Bucks County, PA – Located just 1 1/2 hours from New York City, there are many fun family activities in Bucks County. While there, check out Giggle-berry Fair, a three-story indoor obstacle course; visit Kid's Castle, an eight-story wooden playground with slides, swings, and a treehouse; or take a ride on the New Hope & Ivyland Railroad through the countryside.

Ritu Manoj Jethani / Shutterstock.com

Dorney Park & Wildlife Kingdom – This combination amusement park and water park is fun for all ages. Love roller coasters? This park has seven, along with thrill rides, a carousel, family rides, and kids rides. Located an hour and forty minutes from the city.

Adventureland – In Farmingdale, NY about 1 1/2 hours outside New York City you will discover a traditional amusement park with a mix of roller coasters, carousels, bumper cars, and water rides for children of all ages.

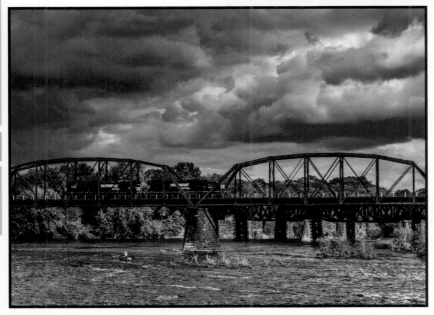

Delaware Rover Railroad Excursions – Do you love trains? Then head across the state line to visit the Delaware Rover Railroad. Ride a real steam train or go on one of their special trips like Thomas & Friends, Dino Days, or the Polar Express. Located about 1 1/2 hours from New York City.

45

Crossword Trivia

Across

3. How many Great Lakes are there?
5. Where does the president live?
6. America's national past time.
9. Where did the Pilgrims first land?
11. In what state was gold first found?
12. Abraham Lincoln was the _____ president.
13. What country gave the Statue of Liberty to America?

Down

1. The longest river in the United States.
2. What state is known as the Lone Star State?
4. The Liberty Bell is located in _____
7. Walt Disney's most famous character.
8. A cold delicious treat on a hot day.
10. Where is Disney World located?

Draw a picture of your favorite memory of the trip.

Trip Journal

Trip Journal

Trip Journal

Trip Journal

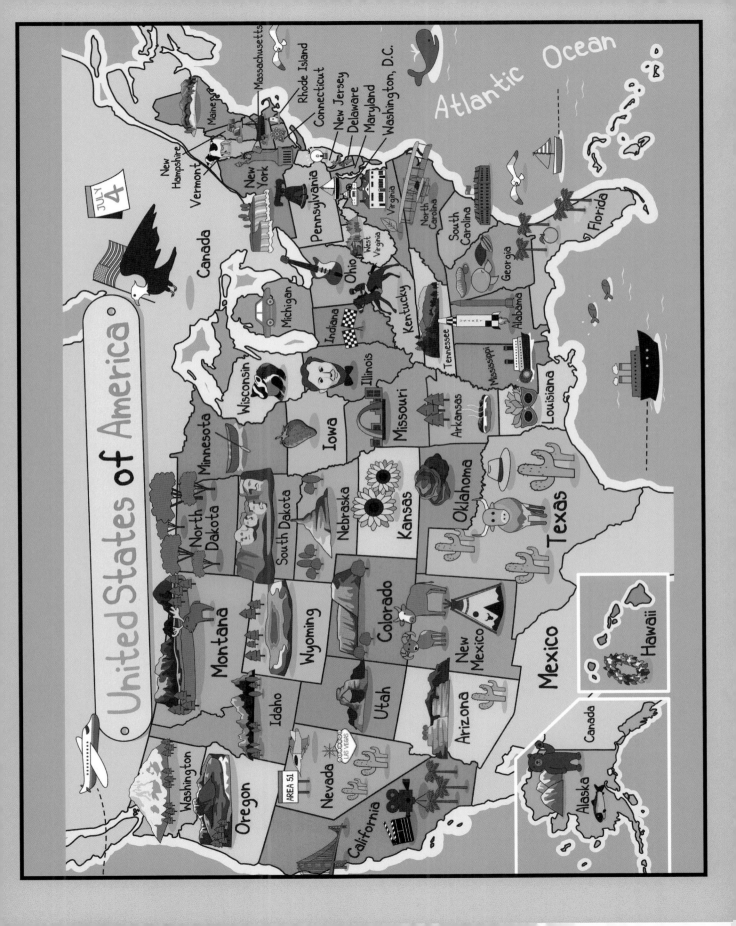

Answers to Puzzles and Games

Across
2. The place you go at the end of your trip
6. Bring this type of book with you when you travel.
8. A green area in a city for people to enjoy.
9. The place you go to catch a plane
9. The number of states in the United States.
10. A type of public transportation that is underground.
11. The thing you carry your belongings in when you travel.

Down
1. Say good _____ when you leave.
4. Another word for vacation.
5. Look at this when you are lost to figure out where to go.
6. When you travel by _____ you might run into traffic.
7. Mode of transportation to get from place to place fast.

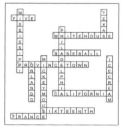

Across
3. How many Great Lakes are there?
5. Where does the president live?
6. America's national past time.
8. Where did the Pilgrims first land?
11. In what state was gold first found?
12. Abraham Lincoln was the _____ president.
13. What country gave the Statue of Liberty to America?

Down
1. The longest river in the United States.
2. What state is known as the Lone Star State?
4. The Liberty Bell is located in _____
7. Walt Disney's most famous character.
9. A cold delicious treat on a hot day.
10. Where is Disney World located?

1. SPRINGFIELD, MASS.
2. YANKEES
3. HOCKEY
4. 1869
5. BOSTON
6. BROOKLYN, NY
7. HOCKEY
8. SALT LAKE CITY
9. BIKING, SWIMMING, RUNNING
10. 26.2 MILES
11. BASKETBALL, TENNIS
12. GOLF
13. BIKE RACE
14. TABLE TENNIS

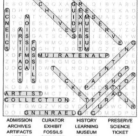

ADMISSION, ARCHIVES, ARTIFACTS, ARTIST, COLLECTION, CURATOR, EXHIBIT, FOSSILS, GIFT SHOP, GUIDE, HISTORY, LEARNING, MUSEUM, PAINTING, PLANETARIUM, PRESERVE, SCIENCE, TICKET, TOUR, VISIT

CAMERA, CHARGER, CLOTHES, JACKET, JOURNAL, PACKING, PAJAMAS, PANTS, SANDALS, SHAMPOO, SHIRT, SHORTS, SNACKS, SNEAKERS, SUITCASE, SUNGLASSES, SUNSCREEN, TOOTHBRUSH, TRAVEL, UMBRELLA

1. ODBWAYAR — Broadway
2. ARLTNEC RPAK — Central Park
3. NATTSE NIDSLA — Staten Island
4. RLBNYKOO — Brooklyn
5. LROEEFRCELK RETENC — Rockefeller Center
6. PEIMER STTEA — Empire State
7. TMHANNAAT — Manhattan
8. ALWL STERET — Wall Street
9. HCEIWRENG — Greenwich
10. TMISE EUSQAR — Times Square

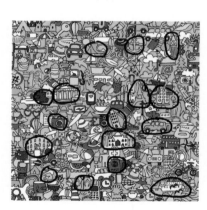

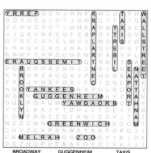

BROADWAY, BROOKLYN, CENTRAL PARK, FERRY, GREENWICH, GUGGENHEIM, HARLEM, LIBERTY, MANHATTAN, SEAPORT, TAXIS, TIMES SQUARE, WALL STREET, YANKEES, ZOO

Printed in Great Britain
by Amazon

23676016R00032